To

Harry,

Wishing you happiness and

for the year 20c

From Stuart.

Keighley

in old picture postcards

by
Ian Dewhirst

European Library – Zaltbommel/Netherlands

Second edition: 1994

GB   ISBN 90 288 4594 1 / CIP

© 1987 European Library – Zaltbommel/Netherlands

INTRODUCTION

The basic history of a town like Keighley is soon told. In 1780 it was a modest market town, whose geographical position – in the Aire Gap, on the North Beck and the River Worth, near the Lancashire border, with developing road and canal communications – ensured its leap ahead with the Industrial Revolution. Between 1801 and 1901 its population rose from 5,745 to 41,564. A wide variety of trades and industries centred round its staple textiles, first cotton then worsted, its manufacture of worsted machinery, machine-tools, mangles, washing and sewing machines.

In the earlier and middle phases of this growth, parts of the older town, unable to cope with sheer numbers of population, deteriorated; there was overcrowding and squalor, ill-health, and early deaths of children. But Victorian virtues and civic determination eventually struggled back towards a balance. A Local Board of Health, formed in 1855, grappled with such necessities as water supply, whilst more especially after 1882 a Borough Council developed Keighley along ambitious lines.

The years between the inauguration of the Borough Council in 1882 and the outbreak of the Great War in 1914 were vital. Councillors tended to be educated, energetic and influential, drawn largely from the dominant mill-owning class, and in three decades they transformed Keighley from a narrow workaday place to a spacious town, still of necessity industrial but imbued with that indefinable sense of graciousness which we now vaguely describe as Edwardian. Streets were widened, ornate stone banks and public buildings erected, avenues of trees planted. To this era belong many of the amenities we now take for granted: parks, library, museum, public transport...

The following photographs show a town in this process of changing from the busy, homely early Victorian to the proud late Victorian and Edwardian, symbolically a shifting of the general centre of gravity from Church Green and the High Street to North Street and Cavendish Street. This transformation was never complete. Smoking mill-chimneys continued to rear above the rooftops, and factories remained interspersed among even some of the best new streets. Horse and cattle fairs occupied at least the side roads into the present century. Hills were always visible in one or more directions, from the very heart of the town.

Housing, to some extent, lagged behind civic developments, for not all the working classes managed to make the step into the decent stone terraces and suburbs which were proliferating by the turn of the century. Westgate and Eastwood Square and the Club-Houses survived for a further generation as reminders of a mid-Victorian past, and it would take the 1930s to fulfil a Council housing ideal.

Victorian development is marked by distinctive buildings, many of which were erected in a spirit of competition. It may not be coincidental that the Parish Church was rebuilt at the same time as the great Temple Street Wesleyan Methodist Chapel, that Dalton Mills followed very soon on the model of nearby Saltaire, that Henry Isaac Butterfield's Cliffe Castle came hard on the heels of his neighbour Isaac Holden's Oakworth House, that the mighty stone banks along North Street are virtually contemporary with one another. Notable, too, is the speed with which the Victorians and their immediate successors worked: whereas the Church Green/High Street/Low Street part of town had grown over centuries, the improved layouts of North Street and Cavendish Street, including nearly all their associated buildings, were accomplished in less than twenty years.

The Great War, though it left Keighley physically intact, tested every aspect of the community. Men went into the forces, and women replaced them in jobs. Industry geared itself to meeting new demands, for shells and field-kitchens, engines for powering searchlights, disinfecting apparatus. The organising ability which manifested itself, as it were naturally, was nothing short of prodigious. People threw themselves into an endless variety of worthy causes and the raising of many funds, under which impetus, despite the exigencies of the time, social life boomed. The town which emerged at the end of 1918 was fully equipped for the advancing twentieth century.

The latter history of Keighley has not been an altogether happy one – but this lies outside our period, and we need not discuss it here. To look back can feel more comfortable.

This collection of photographs could not have been brought together without the kindness and co-operation of many individuals and several organisations. The considerable Local Collection of Keighley Reference Library has provided the backbone with 3, 5, 6, 7, 8, 9, 11, 14, 15, 23, 26, 37, 40, 48, 51, 53, 66, 67, 72 and 75. I am also indebted to the Cliffe Castle Art Gallery and Museum, Keighley, for 31 and 33, and to the 'Keighley News' for 76. The remainder are from the author's collection, accumulated over the years through the generosity of very many people. Special thanks must go to Mr. N.K. Howarth, A.B.I.P.P., who supplied 36 and who for nearly three decades has been bringing out the 'latent image' in so many of my faded originals.

1. Dedicated to St. Andrew, Keighley Parish Church was built between 1846 and 1848. With seating for 1,400 and designed by the architect of Leeds Parish Church, R.D. Chantrell, this was the third church in less than half a century to occupy its central site, its predecessors having been demolished in 1805 and 1846 respectively. The clock in the tower was presented by parishioner Joseph Greenwood in 1903, and set going on the occasion of his seventy-fifth birthday. This postcard probably dates from 1904, during the laying of electric tram-lines in Church Street or, as it has become more popularly known, Church Green. The inn on the right, the Lord Rodney, is Keighley's oldest public house. Originally the Old Red Lion, its name was changed to commemorate Lord Rodney's victory over the Spanish fleet in 1780.

2. Church Street in 1890, the traditional heart of Keighley from its earliest known days. On the right, hailed in its time as 'one of the most important and extensive schemes for street improvement', is the new crescent built by Alderman Richard Longden Hattersley. This formed a handsome frontage to his foundry, and was intended to comprise ten shops, eighteen upstairs offices and a re-constituted Crown Hotel. In the event, fourteen 'lofty' rooms were occupied by the Keighley Conservative Club (Alderman Hattersley being a leading Conservative), complete with a mahogany bar and facilities for billiards, card playing and smoking. The tracks are for horse-trams, which commenced operations in 1889.

3. The old Crown Hotel in Church Green. This and adjacent properties were bought up by Keighley Corporation in 1884, when the carriageway was a scant ten feet wide, the buildings being demolished and Church Green widened five years later. The tall elaborate drinking-fountain on the left was presented to the town in 1869 by Miss Butterfield of Cliffe Hall, as a means of innocently quenching the thirst of some who might otherwise have been tempted by the plentiful hostelries in this locality! The fountain (which had occupied the approximate site of Keighley's former stocks) was transferred into the new Devonshire Park on its opening in 1888.

4. An unknown local postcard producer cashes in on a topical event, capturing a blurred because mobile General Booth being driven down the High Street on 12th August 1905. The leader of the Salvation Army spent a weekend in Keighley during his 'great northward motor-car tour'. People thronged the streets to cheer as he passed, and for two days the town was given over to Salvation Army activities. 'The familiar 'Blood and Fire' uniform was met with everywhere,' observed the local press. The General was given a civic reception at the Municipal Hall, and the Queen's Theatre was placed at his disposal for two packed Sunday meetings, proceedings at which were 'very enthusiastic'.

5. The High Street, as its name suggests one of Keighley's older streets, about the turn of the century. The imposing four-storey premises on the corner at the right – Central Buildings of 1898 – illustrate the contrast between Keighley's late Victorian development and an earlier, more modest yet stylistically pleasing townscape. Beyond Central Buildings, the junction of High Street/Low Street and Church Green/North Street, still colloquially called the Cross, used to mark the centre of Keighley parish, which comprised a one-mile radius from this point. Notable among businesses in this scene are the Exchange Vaults and Simon Billows and Co., newsagents and stationers who doubled as agents for the British and Foreign Bible Society.

6. This comparatively open space at the upper end of the High Street was commonly known as 't'Top o't-'Town'. Isaac Emmott, the fruit and potato merchant, was also a wholesale dealer in 'rough salt, rock salt, and salt for domestic purposes'. This photograph, taken about 1890, is interesting because of its bystanders, including a policeman striking a pose. Keighley's police, like those of many towns, had a chequered history, through parish constables and night watchmen to a force recruited by the Local Board of Health. The Superintendent of the latter was rather dauntingly 'held responsible for the peace of the district, and for the lives and the property therein'. In 1857, the inauguration of the West Riding Constabulary had transferred police duties into the understandably more capable hands of a regular force.

7. In common with many towns involved in the Industrial Revolution, Keighley's population grew rapidly. Its 5,745 inhabitants of 1801 (when, even then, antiquarian Thomas Dunham Whitaker had complained of 'the din of recent population'), had become 18,258 by 1851, and 33,540 by 1881. Inevitably, overcrowding affected such residential areas as Westgate, originally a not unpleasant district with gardens and orchards alongside the North Beck. 'Formerly Westgate, with the North Beck meandering through it,' wrote one commentator in 1903, 'was one of the beauty spots of the town, but alas! Utilitarian ideas have sadly changed its aspect.' This photograph shows Quebec Bridge, at the very crux of old residential Keighley. In 1867 it had been estimated that the North Beck had raised its bed by four to five feet with rubbish accumulated during the previous 35 years! The whole area was demolished between the wars.

8. The Ginnel, near Quebec Bridge. This scene illustrates the type of dwellings, sometimes crowded as many as 66 to the acre, replaced by Corporation houses – twelve to the acre – from the later 1920s. In 1908 a journalist was describing 'windows where paper and rags have replaced some of the panes, and... doors with panels broken and the beading stripped off. Some of the doors bear visible signs of vicious blows or kicks'. Some dwellings had 'hardly any furniture, boxes, etc., being often utilised'. Victorian and Edwardian death rates in such areas could be nearly double those of the town as a whole.

9. Turn-of-the-century Westgate, the street which gave its name to a locality, with the Bay Horse Inn on the left, denoted by the lamp. Year after year, Keighley's Medical Officer of Health spelled out the shortcomings of homes such as these: 'it was notorious that on some no direct ray of sunlight had fallen since the houses were built 100 years ago, in all there was a complete absence of keeping-cellars, some had rat-infested cupboards, in others food-stuffs were kept under the bed, wash-houses there were none, coals were stored anyhow, anywhere, and as for closet accommodation, some, indeed, had water-closets, others had tub-closets, single or joint, all were a nuisance...' It is against scenes such as this that the achievements of the present century should be measured.

10. This is another of Keighley's oldest thoroughfares, Low Street, decorated for the Coronation of King Edward VII in 1902. The flag-bedecked shop on the right belonged to manufacturing confectioners Messrs. J. Bottomley and Sons, Ltd. This firm, surviving the murder at Leeds in 1883 of its founder, Jonas Bottomley, was by the turn of the century producing over twenty tons of sweets a week from its factory in adjoining Adelaide Street. Especially famous were Bottomleys' lime fruit tablets and mint rock, the subject of extravagant claims. 'The greatest enemy to Bronchitis!' cried Bottomleys' mint rock advertising. 'Saves Thousands of Lives from that dreadful disease.'

11. Described at the time as 'the most picturesque survival of eighteenth-century Keighley,' the Fleece Hotel – formerly the Golden Fleece – in Low Street, was demolished in 1934 to make way for a new Marks and Spencer 'super stores' which opened the following March. This hostelry had been a recurring name in the town's social history. In the 1820s it had served as meetingplace for a woolcombers' club (an early form of trade union). During the coaching era, travellers had set out from the Fleece, aboard the 'Royal Alexander' for Leeds, the 'Tradesman' for Bradford, or the 'Wonder' for Halifax. After its demolition, one of its interior doors – symbolic of its many uses – was found to have had, at different times, no less than eight keyholes.

12. 'A bit of Old Keighley' rather wistfully runs the caption on this 1930-ish postcard of a little newsagent's and stationer's shop with a bow window in Changegate – the older name by which the top end of Low Street was still known into the present century. There was a Thomas Crabtree selling books in Changegate in the 1830s (he supplied the Mechanics' Institute Library in its early years), whilst the firm printed hundreds of posters during the middle decades of the nineteenth century. In common with so much old property, 'Crabtree's' succumbed to between-the-wars developments.

MARKET PLACE, KEIGHLEY.

13. In 1305 Edward I granted Keighley's Market Charter to Henry de Keighley, whose family remained Lords of the Manor for fifteen generations until a sixteenth-century daughter of the last male of the line married a Cavendish of the Dukes of Devonshire. For more than 500 years the market was held on Church Green, but moved on to this purpose-built site in 1833, occupying it till 1971. The Market still holds an important place in working-class memories – most veterans recall late Saturday-night shopping excursions when perishable foodstuffs were sold off cheap. This is the view along Market Street towards Low Street. The heavily-loaded pole above the roof-tops marks the then telephone exchange.

14. North Street immediately prior to its widening and virtual re-building in the 1890s, looking towards Church Green and the Cross – so named, not because it makes a cross-roads with High Street and Low Street, but because the old Market Cross used to stand there. Originally laid out in 1786, North Street at the Cross marked the beginning of the Keighley and Kendal Turnpike Road. The horse-tram lines had been laid in 1889 by a Keighley Tramways Company which operated a frequent service between Ingrow and Utley. The horses also went on duty with the Fire Brigade when need arose!

15. North Street in 1890, with the great Lockwood and Mawson Mechanics' Institute contrasting with small wooden shops. One of the houses on the left had been built by machine-maker George Smith in 1852, when more solid citizens were moving out of the traditional residential centre of town into a new suburbia beginning to creep out along North Street. Stone came from local quarries at Hainworth Shaw and Bracken Bank, flags from Wicken Crag and Penistone at Haworth. George Smith's house was furnished with a rather grand water-closet with deal 'elbows' and a mahogany seat; there was also a privy with a seat '20 inches wide with two holes', and for good measure, out in the yard, a urinal of strong flags six feet high. By coincidence, George Smith's house was destined in 1902 to adjoin the site of Keighley's Carnegie Public Library of which his son, Sir Swire Smith, had been an instigator.

16. Examples of the fine new buildings, embellished with highly decorative stone-carving, which graced the reconstructed North Street of the late nineteenth century. To the right of the shops of M. and E. Stell and Mrs. Fred Pearson is the Bradford District Bank Limited, erected in 1892 on the site of a private residence, boasting frontages on both North Street and Chapel Lane. Its architects were W. and J.B. Bailey of Keighley. Joseph Booth Bailey had earlier been an assistant with the great Bradford architects Lockwood and Mawson. He and his brother, Wilson Bailey, were responsible for many Keighley buildings of the period, being equally competent with mills, churches, shops and houses. Their most noteworthy work included All Saints' Church, the Temperance Institute, and Victoria Hospital.

North Street.

Keighley.

Pub. by the Skipton Stationery Co., Skipton.

17. The superb vista looking northwards from the Cross by the beginning of this century. The long handsome block of shop frontages along the right-hand side is Burlington Buildings of 1891. The shop in the right foreground, in addition to being a Midland Railway and Cook's Tours booking office, also operates as a shipping and emigration agency. Many men emigrated from Keighley, especially in times of industrial depression, sending for their families once they had settled in the New World. In the mid-1850s, for example, emigrants could apply for weekly sailings 'to America, Australia, or any of the British Colonies'. By the late 1870s, New Zealand was a popular choice.

18. The spacious view northwards along North Street during the second decade of this century, typically dominated by the clock-tower of the Lockwood and Mawson Mechanics' Institute of 1870. Gracious buildings along the left-hand side include respectively the Police Station of 1887, the Public Library of 1904, and the Temperance Institute of 1896, the two latter distinguished by cupolas. Civic developments, which enjoyed a peak between the 1890s and the Great War, encompassed the planting of trees to provide an avenue along North Street. Keighley's electric trams had a comparatively short life, and would be discontinued in 1924. Incidentally, this postcard mistakenly describes this as Skipton Road, which in reality North Street does not become until beyond the furthest point of this scene.

MECHANIC'S INSTITUTE, KEIGHLEY.

19. One of the new electric trams in North Street, backed by the Keighley Mechanics' Institute, the town's physical focal point. A work of the famous partnership of Bradford architects, Henry Francis Lockwood and William Mawson, this had officially opened in 1870 and had been enlarged in 1887. The clock was added to its tower in 1892, the gift of industrialist Prince Smith. Keighley Mechanics' Institute, which also accommodated the School of Science and Art and the Trade and Grammar School, served for ninety years as an educational and social centre. From its inception, it brought a library, newsroom and gymnasium within reach of all, and its Christmas Conversaziones were enjoyed alike by 'Tories and Radicals, Churchmen and Dissenters'. Much of the building was burnt out in 1962.

20. The Mechanics' Institute clock-tower looked stately from all angles. Here, about 1905, it completes the vista down Highfield Lane and Albert Street. In the left foreground is the Albert Street Baptist Chapel, erected in 1865 'in the Byzantine style, freely treated'; beyond, the Temperance Institute of 1896. This important social centre comprised a large hall seating 800, a lower hall for 350, and a variety of smaller rooms: in the 1930s the building was accommodating at least 1,800 meetings a year. On the right are the Public Baths which had originated in 1876 after a seven-year controversy which had split ratepayers into two camps, bathites and anti-bathites.

21. The southward view along North Street on an August day in 1902, with the Parish Church tower just visible at the end of the vista. The current widening of the street has left lamp-posts temporarily out in the road! The view is naturally dominated by the Mechanics' Institute. The end building of the nearer group on the left, at an angle to the corner, was Sandywood House. This had been built as a cotton mill in the early 1800s, later becoming a boarding school for young ladies, then the home of the Sandywood Bowling Club. There was a bowling green round the back of the premises, on the site of the former mill dam.

SKIPTON ROAD, KEIGHLEY (2)

22. North Street (again ambiguously called Skipton Road on this postcard) looking northwards out of town. Changing habits of the twentieth century have produced a garage and bicycle shop on the left, and the Picture House on the right, complete with its ornate glass canopy. Opened in 1913, one of eight cinemas which Keighley was to boast (though never quite all at once), the Picture House was billed as 'the House of Luxury and Comfort'. Patrons in 'the body of the hall' sat in 300 'armchairs' at threepence each and another 300 at sixpence; the Grand Circle cost ninepence and a shilling. There were a café and an orchestra of four, and the vestibule had 'mahogany panelled walls and an Italian mosaic pavement'. As for the 'operating equipment', this was 'thoroughly modern, and comprises two of Butcher's No. 12 Empire machines, by means of which long intervals between pictures will be obviated'.

23. Showfield about 1890, its skyline dominated by the fairytale turrets of Cliffe Castle, when this represented a growing fashionable side of town. Good terrace houses are being built down Strawberry Street, and more substantial residences are spreading out along Skipton Road, individually named – Ashville, Springfield, North and Earl Villas. The chapel-like building in the foreground is in fact the Drake and Tonson's Girls' Grammar School, named after local educational benefactors John Drake and Jonas Tonson and opened on this site in 1872. The land on the right of this scene was used literally as a show field, where visiting circuses and other spectacles would pitch their marquees.

24. An early twentieth-century view to the north-east from the Parish Church tower, across the roofs of Changegate to Cooke Lane and Townfield Gate and an area now largely demolished and replaced by a 1960s town centre. Older higgledy-piggledy property contrasts with handsome recent buildings, including the School Board Offices (1893), the New Queen's Theatre (1900), and the Gas Offices and Showrooms (1902). Town centre factories range in name from the exotic Honduras Works to the more mundane Airedale Works. Far back on the left rises the graceful spire of the United Methodist Free Church in Cavendish Street.

COOK LANE, KEIGHLEY.

25. Prior to the laying out of North Street in 1786, Cooke Lane (there has always been an ambiguity about its spelling, with or without an *e*) served as Keighley's main north-south thoroughfare. This is the view from the Low Street corner in the early 1900s. Premises along the left-hand side include the Old Brewery of Aaron King and Co., whilst beyond, a funeral cortege stands outside William Harris's livery stables. On the right are the imposing Gas Offices, with Stanley's Stores in the foreground. Highly respected Stanley's Stores specialised in such justifiable treats as 'Invalids' Champagne and 'Stanley's Golden-Glen Glenlivet', which carried the heartening encomium: 'Where Whiskey is needed as a medicine this is highly recommended by the medical faculty.' This entire vista disappeared under Keighley's 1960s shopping precinct.

26. Townfield Gate, about 1890. In the left background looms the United Methodist Free Church, and on the far right the roof of the Queen's Theatre. Townfield probably represented a medieval system of communal land cultivation, which had been largely enclosed in 1790. What remains in this photograph was used for open-air meetings, to which local residents objected. Matters came to a head in 1905, when an angry house-holder hired an organ-grinder to disrupt an al-fresco gathering of the Keighley Temperance Society. This tactic ensured an audience of a thousand for the next temperance meeting, but this time the diversion was provided by a cheap-jack from Sheffield, who 'proceeded to drink beer from bottles'. Keighley Corporation decided to provide another open-air site, and the Town Hall Square was the result. Eventually Townfield Gate became used as a bus terminus, until the fully-fledged Bus Station came into being.

27. Cavendish Street, showing its notorious 'bottle-neck' between the Oddfellows' Arms on the left and the Queen's Head Inn on the right. 1899 saw the start of a scheme to make Cavendish Street 'a close rival to North Street for architectural effect, width and symmetry', and indifferent premises, down the left-hand background as seen here, were demolished. The Corporation had sold the Oddfellows' Arms to Halifax brewers T. Ramsden and Sons Ltd. on condition that they replace it with a finer hostelry: the Cavendish Hotel was the result. The Queen's Head Inn was allowed to remain in business only until the Cavendish Hotel was completed, then in turn demolished. After its virtual re-building, Cavendish Street was 22 yards wide.

KEIGHLEY, CAVENDISH STREET.

28. This is the spacious view up Cavendish Street which by the early 1900s was intended to impress the visitor emerging from Keighley's railway station. On the left, the Victoria Hotel catered primarily for commercial travellers. Its novelties included a hydraulic lift, electric lights 'most artistically arranged', and a grand restaurant and buffet; it could also lay on balls and public banquets. On the right, Cavendish Street shoppers are protected by a stylish glass canopy. Thirty-six of these handsome shops had been built by Sir Prince Smith, textile manufacturer and director of the Bradford District Bank.

29. Cavendish Street, from the former bottle-neck, about 1920. Again, the Mechanics' Institute dominates. The spire on its nearer side belonged to the United Methodist Free Church (this denomination had originally seceded from the Wesleyans during a dispute over an organ) which opened in 1868 and was nicknamed the 'Cock Chapel' in honour of its weathercock, which crowed 125 feet above the street on top of the highest spire in Keighley. On the left, the tall building with turret provided a fine headquarters for the Keighley Cycling Club in 1896; but optician J.E. Gledhill's shop on the corner was to be replaced in 1923 by a Halifax Building Society in Portland stone.

30. The view from the upper windows of the Craven Bank, North Street, a little after noon on 23rd January 1900. Wooden shops and hoardings surround the Corporation stone-yard, destined a few years later to provide the site for a spacious Town Hall Square. Factories have let their workers out half-an-hour early in order to watch an Active Service Contingent of the 3rd Volunteer Battalion, Duke of Wellington's (West Riding) Regiment, march off along North Street en route for the Boer War. The Battalion band leads. Behind them, distinguishable by their greatcoats and the khaki covers on their helmets, come the 36 men bound for the front. The picture was taken by an amateur photographer, a gentleman 'of a quiet and unassuming disposition' called Taylor Smith.

31. Another photograph which can be precisely dated – thanks to the hoardings advertising a visit of Buffalo Bill Cody's Wild West show on 7th October 1903 – gives the view across the Corporation stone-yard from the opposite side on Cooke Street. In the right background looms the Mechanics' Institute clock-tower; whilst along from middle to left runs the Carnegie Free Library in process of erection. The awning over its front entrance marks where master craftsman Alex. F. Smith, responsible for much decorative work around the town, was producing arguably his finest piece of stone-carving. This picture, with its contrast between handsome buildings and utilitarian clutter, symbolises again a community emerging with civic pride from haphazard origins.

32. This Keighley vista from the south-east stresses the industrial nature of the Victorian town. According to a memorial presented to the Earl of Beaconsfield in 1878, about the time that this photograph was taken, Keighley boasted seventy worsted factories, 'containing 301,580 spinning and doubling spindles, and 6,452 looms'. In other words, Keighley was estimated to possess 'one-tenth of the mills, nearly one-eighth of the spindles, and nearly one-twelfth of the looms employed in the worsted trade throughout the United Kingdom'. Other manufactures included steam-engines, lathes, sewing machines, and washing and wringing machines – some 64,000 of the latter were produced in a single year. Notwithstanding, the Earl of Beaconsfield was not persuaded to grant Keighley parliamentary borough status on that occasion.

33. The original of this postcard, showing children coming out of Haggas's mill at Ingrow, was meticulously dated twelve noon on 22nd August 1908 – this was a Saturday, so they have finished work for the weekend. By this period, these factory children would be protected by legislation: they will have started work only at the age of eleven and on condition that they have attained minimum standards in reading, writing and arithmetic, and they will work first as half-timers (half the day at the mill and half at school). They will begin working full-time when they are thirteen. Their first jobs in the spinning department will be doffing (removing full bobbins and replacing them with empty ones) and piecing (twisting broken threads together).

34. Damems Mill continued to depend on water long after industry had moved on to other sources of power. Built, like so many early Keighley factories, originally for cotton manufacture, Damems Mill – again typically – changed to worsted. Water from the River Worth was diverted into the dam seen here, from which it could be discharged over a bridge (dated 1842) and down a sluice to a water-wheel housed in the building in the left foreground. The wheel was 26 feet 6 inches in diameter and its blades were 12 feet wide. It could produce a maximum of 80 horse-power. In 1936 this traditional source was still turning nearly a hundred looms.

35. Dalton Mills, seen here when new in the 1870s, demonstrating that not all factories were necessarily dark and satanic. The Midland Railway runs across the foreground, and beyond, fringed by trees on the nearer side of the mills, flows the River Worth. One of J. and J. Craven's works, Dalton Mills enjoyed two noteworthy features: viz. the largest mill beam engine in the world, capable of developing over 2,000 horse-power and taking seven years to build; and a look-out tower round its chimney. This latter was the inspiration of Joseph H. Craven, whose adjoining Strong Close House occupied low ground and had no views. To the left of Dalton Mills can be seen St. Mary's Church, built in 1855 for the Parish of Eastwood.

36. Fleece Mills, a town centre industrial complex, seen here about 1905 behind the less fashionable side of Cavendish Street. The original Fleece Mill was built by William Sugden about 1819, and shortly afterwards became the first factory in Keighley to be lit with gas; the premises grew during the century. Some of the single-storey businesses in the foreground are trading on their address: there is a Cavendish Hosiery, and boot and leather merchant Albert Massey patented 'Cavendish Felt Socks' for keeping the feet warm in winter. On the far right is the Victoria Steam Laundry, wherein one over-awed witness of the time noted 'huge piles of bundles of wearing apparel, including collars, cuffs, cravats, blouses, aprons, shirts, singlets, handkerchiefs & c.,' to say nothing of a profusion of table-cloths, blankets, sheets and antimacassars. One of this laundry's period slogans ran: 'Gentlemen's Linen got up equal to new.'

37. This Becks Road factory, seen here in the early stages of its construction, was built for worsted spinners Robert Clough and Co. It was started in August of 1908 and finished in March the following year – an extensive six-storey premises, complete with chimney and dam, straddling the North Beck. On the left beyond the mill rise the tall houses of Westgate, whilst behind the growing stump of chimney lies the congested Damside, both areas cleared within the next thirty years. Robert Clough himself epitomised those many manufacturers whose interests extended to their communities, for he was deeply involved in the Infants' Aid Society, the YMCA and the NSPCC. At 34, he served as Keighley's then youngest Mayor in 1907, and was elected Keighley's first Conservative Member of Parliament (his predecessors had all been Liberals) in the Coalition government of 1919. He was knighted in 1921.

38. Ingrow Fold, rare seventeenth-century buildings surviving until comparatively recently within a mile of Keighley town centre. The date carved above the main doorway was 1663, and the door itself was thought to be the original, heavily studded with wooden pegs, one of the best examples of its type in the district. The cottages fell vacant in 1957 and were demolished three years later – the barns had already gone. This photograph was taken about 1913 by Dr. Francis Villy, a medical practitioner better remembered for his work as an amateur archaeologist, especially for his investigation of the courses of Roman roads. A trowel and the letters S.P.Q.R. are fittingly incorporated on his gravestone.

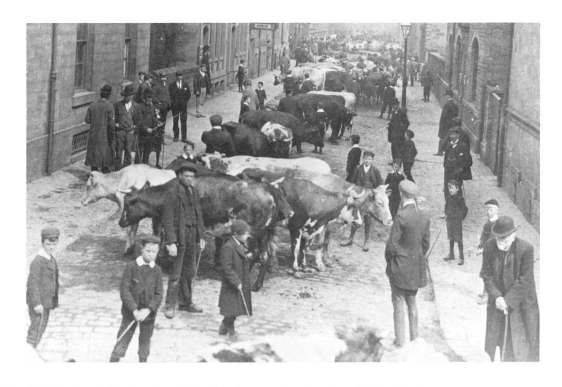

39. A reminder of Keighley's agricultural past, continuing into the present century: the cattle fair in Scott Street, parallel and within a stone's-throw of North Street. Keighley fair had been traditionally held, by the terms of its Market Charter of 1305, 'on the eve on the day and on the day following of St. Simon and St. Jude', but by the early 1900s, when this postcard was produced, the time was probably May. Increasing traffic had by then pushed livestock out of the main thoroughfares into side roads. It was the custom for cows to stand for sale in Scott Street, Russell Street and Devonshire Street, horses at the bottom of West Lane, and sheep round the back of the High Street. Afterwards, it is said, the Fire Brigade would clean the streets with their hoses!

40. This cooper, still working in crumbling old premises in Chapel Lane in 1926, provides a reminder of the variety of trades formerly carried on in the town. In the 1880s, for example, in addition to staple industries and every expected line of business, Keighley also boasted manufacturers of such diverse commodities as washing liquid, grease, aerated water, cart covers, venetian blinds, dry soap, mattresses and bedding, brushes, coaches, railway wagons, tobacco and umbrellas; to say nothing of specialist occupations like a tripe dresser, a herring curer, a japanner, a taxidermist, and a 'bone setter, and dealer in cattle spice'.

41. In 1901 Keighley possessed no less than seventeen slaughter-houses. Situated in the heart of Westgate, this (surprisingly) more substantial example was mercifully replaced by a new municipal abattoir in 1930. During their last full year of operation, however, these premises witnessed the killing of 2,392 cattle, 153 calves, 2,086 pigs and 7,059 sheep. A total of 96 cattle and 26 pigs were found to be infected with tuberculosis. Here boys begged bladders to use as footballs. The iron ring visible in the ground towards the bottom left-hand corner was used, in conjunction with a chain, to pull a cow's head down to the ground in order to strike it with the poleaxe.

42. The teachings of Emanuel Swedenborg gained early adherents in Keighley, which in 1789 formed the first Swedenborgian – or New Jerusalem – Society in Yorkshire. Their temple or meeting-house was built in 1805 in King Street where Acres Mill, belonging to member Berry Smith, adjoined and eventually expanded round it. Yet for most of the century this remained a peaceful corner, embellished with a text from Swedenborg above the door: 'All religion hath relation to life, and the life of religion is to do good.' By 1891, when they moved into more ambitious premises in Devonshire Street, the Keighley Swedenborgians mustered 63 members, with 62 scholars and 24 teachers in their Sunday School. They also ran a sick club and a library of 500 volumes. Secretary for many years was Alfred Bottomley, father of the Georgian poet and playwright Gordon Bottomley.

43. Temple Street Wesleyan Methodist Chapel opened in 1846, coinciding with the re-building of the Parish Church. Its architect was James Simpson, of Leeds. Keighley Methodists had occupied this site since their earliest days, their first chapel in 1754 having replaced gardens and orchards in what was still a small rustic town. James Simpson's chapel could seat nearly 1,600, but crammed 2,000 in for its opening service. Originally set imposingly back from North Street, Temple Street Chapel could scarcely hope to maintain its spacious setting indefinitely in an expanding town; although its Trustees tried planting 'forest trees on the plot of ground in front of the Chapel'. This photograph was probably taken immediately prior to the substantial re-building of North Street in the 1890s.

44. St. Peter's Church, formed appropriately on St. Peter's Day in 1872, was one of several later Victorian measures 'to provide for the spiritual wants of the large and increasing population of the Parish of Keighley', notably in a growing suburbia. For its first ten years, St. Peter's worshipped in an iron building, until this church 'in the early English style of architecture', accommodating 850, opened in Halifax Road. The iron building thereupon became a Sunday School. St. Peter's epitomised the range of social, as well as religious, amenities offered by places of worship in their hey-day. In addition to the Sunday services, a typical week offered a savings bank, sewing party, Men's and Women's Help Societies, Bible and singing classes, a Band of Hope, Church Temperance Society and Mothers' Union. St. Peter's Church was demolished in 1956.

45. The Church of St. John the Evangelist was consecrated for the newly-formed parish of Ingrow-cum-Hainworth in 1843, in time to serve as Keighley's temporary Parish Church during the re-building of the latter between 1846 and 1848. Due to the rather curious boundaries appertaining at the time, 1,676 Ingrow residents lived technically in Keighley and 2,344 in Bingley. This view can be dated around the turn of the century, as the Ingrow Board Schools, farther back on the left of the church, are in process of erection. The Keighley and Worth Valley Railway occupies the foreground. The waggons bear the initials of the Midland Railway – from which the Worth Valley line was a branch – or the names of individual collieries and coal dealers.

46. The Town Hall Livery Stables in North Street, including an ornate hearse. Cab proprietor Joseph Smith, who had started out as a greengrocer with a donkey and cart, built up an 'excellently-appointed' establishment of thirty horses and a fleet of waggonettes, gigs, landaus, hearses, wedding and mourning coaches (funerals provided a speciality). The horses were stabled on the upper floor, and entered the building by means of a ramp at the front entrance. A nearby bell-pull was guaranteed to summon attention by day or night, since transport was available at all hours. In 1920 this site was occupied by the Regent Picture House.

47. Turn-of-the-century Christmas fare displayed outside the Keighley Industrial Co-operative Society's Central Stores in Brunswick Street. The boards beside the door read respectively: 'Your Smallest Order will Receive our Closest Attention. Try Us' and 'Look B 4 U Leap. This is the Place for Poultry.' A working-class enterprise, the Keighley Co-operative Society had been launched in 1860. Early Committee members had tramped over to Hebden Bridge for cheaper flour, and the first treasurer used to hide the takings each night in his linen-chest. But by the time the Brunswick Street Stores were built, they replaced 'fifteen cottages, a van house, a large workshop and yard'. Their opening in 1886 was celebrated appropriately by a lantern lecture on 'Co-operative Thrift'.

48. Keighley Public Library, officially opened by the Duke of Devonshire in 1904. This was the first library in England to benefit from the generosity of Andrew Carnegie, who gave £10,000 towards it. Keighley reciprocated by becoming the first town in England to confer the Freedom of its Borough on Mr. Carnegie, whose gift was occasioned through his friendship with the Keighley educationalist Sir Swire Smith. The design for the Carnegie Free Library, as it was then called, was based on 'a free treatment of Early Renaissance'. It incorporated the bookstock of the former Keighley Mechanics' Institute Library founded in 1825. When it opened in 1904, it comprised a lending library, reading room, patents library and students' room; a reference library would follow in 1912, and a children's library in 1929.

**READING ROOM,
CARNEGIE FREE LIBRARY, KEIGHLEY.**

49. Studious citizens in the reading room of the Carnegie Free Library – a uniformed curator stood by to maintain silence! – posing for the benefit of fashionable Keighley photographers Hall and Siggers. There was seating for 150, and the walls were embellished with some of Mr. Carnegie's favourite quotations, such as 'They are never alone who are accompanied by noble thoughts' and 'The chief glory of a nation is its authors'. When this reading room opened in 1904, it took twenty daily newspapers, 80 weeklies, 63 monthly magazines and two quarterlies. The 'Phonetic Journal' on the foreground table is a reminder of one of Keighley's special interests: the first Esperanto Society in England was formed here in 1902.

50. The Keighley Fire Brigade, probably in a Friendly Societies' Gala procession around the turn of the century. They are passing St. Peter's Church in Halifax Road. Keighley's Fire Brigade had originated modestly in 1829, when six part-time firemen were paid four shillings a year, plus six-pence an hour when attending fires, and were allowed to beg at Christmas! By the time of this photograph, however, the Brigade was commanded by the legendary Captain Smith Lonsdale, whose career spanned forty years and more than 450 fires. The leading vehicle is the double cylinder steam fire engine which Keighley had acquired in 1893.

51. Keighley's Gas Works at Thwaites, opened in 1876. The town had been lit by gas since 1825, but fifty years later the growing population required a larger scale of operations. The new Thwaites site included a section of old river course utilised for tipping, and adjoined the railway from which elevated sidings led into the retort house and coal stores. The offices and laboratories boasted a decorative clock tower; there were also a dining-room and baths for the workmen. After the official opening, the Chairman of the Local Board entertained guests to dinner and a menu of hare soup, turbot, calf's head, pigeon pie, pheasants and partridge. Meanwhile, the Gas Committee provided a supper for 'the whole of the employees of the Gas Department'.

52. East Riddlesden Hall, arguably Keighley's most attractive historical building, is seen here about 1900. The Canons of Bolton Priory were buying fish from its pond as early as 1320. The Hall itself dates from the seventeenth century, and a later tenant reared the Airedale Heifer, one of those heavy-weight creatures which the 1800s set such store by. The fate of East Riddlesden Hall was to hang in the balance in 1933, when it was threatened with demolition, but happily it was bought by brothers Alderman William Anderton Brigg and County Alderman J.J. Brigg, who promptly handed it over to the National Trust.

53. The classical frontage of Eastwood House, built in 1819 by worsted manufacturer William Sugden of Fleece Mill. Its extensive parkland, half a mile east of the town proper, occupied a 'field of plain earth' where horseraces had been run in the early eighteenth century. Part of the Eastwood House estate disappeared under housing developments; the rest was bought by public subscription and opened as Victoria Park in 1893. This photograph was probably taken a short time earlier, before the courtyard behind Eastwood House was covered over to form a large hall accommodating a four-month Science and Art Exhibition to mark the Park's official opening. In reality, Keighley's museum was to remain here for more than sixty years, Eastwood House having become better known as the Mansion House.

Cliffe Castle

Valentines Series

54. Undoubtedly Keighley's grandest residence, Cliffe Castle, built by manufacturer Henry Isaac Butterfield over a decade from 1875. Described at the time as 'a modernised Tudor castle in the Victorian era', Cliffe Castle sported a fine conservatory and winter gardens, and such arrogant details as a bronze lamp-post before its entrance porch, 'the facsimile of those that adorn the Thames Embankment, except that Mr. Butterfield's crest is substituted for the Royal crown'! Interior features included Rossini's bed, 'a tea-caddy belonging to the late Emperor of France', and Chinese vases looted from the Chinese Emperor's summer palace in Peking. In 1950, Cliffe Castle and its extensive grounds were bought and given to the town by Sir Bracewell Smith, a native of Keighley and former Lord Mayor of London.

55. The turrets of Cliffe Castle seen beyond the 'ornamental serpentine lake' of a new Devonshire Park. This was Keighley's first public park, laid out on nine acres of land presented to the town by the Duke of Devonshire. It included the obligatory Victorian bandstand and a terrace promenade commanding 'a magnificent view of the valley of the Aire, with Rombalds Moor in the distance'. 20,000 Sunday School scholars, teachers and townsfolk celebrated the Queen's 1887 Jubilee there, although the park was not officially opened until 1888, an event commemorated in rhyme by Keighley's unofficial poet laureate, William Wright or Bill o'th'Hoylus End: *This bonny little garden/ Is fine for perambulators,/ Where our handsome servant-lasses/ Can wheel our lovely creatures,/ And oh! how happy they will be!/ As time they are beguiling,/ When the mammy and the daddy/ Are upon the babies smiling.*

56. The Queen's Theatre and Opera House was rebuilt by Edward Darbey in 1889 in brick and stone on the site of an original American-style five-storey wooden theatre of 1880. Its gallery seated 1,000, its pit 500, its side circle 200 and its centre circle 100. A further 300 sat – on chairs imported from Austria – in the pit stalls, and there were six private boxes. The staple fare was melodrama, with titles like 'A Woman's Wrongs', 'False Lights', 'Passion's Slave', 'Bells of Fate'. This theatre enjoyed a comparatively short life, being superseded in 1900 by one designed by the great theatre architect Frank Matcham, sadly demolished in its turn in 1961.

57. Inns have played an important part in the town's social life, none more so than the Queen Street Arms (colloquially the 'Grinning Rat'), seen here when the late Victorian licensee was Luke Parker, who doubled as a blacksmith. The Queen Street Arms boasted theatrical connections. When a Keighley Thespian Society was formed in 1848, they met 'in Old Joe Walbank's beer house, later The Grinning Rat'. From 1903 the publican was Jabez Wood, formerly manager of the nearby Queen's Theatre; he was followed by his daughter and son-in-law. Actors would rehearse in a back room, and the inn's nickname may have originated from a company who frequented it while appearing in a play called 'The Grinning Rat'. The Queen Street Arms closed its doors for the last time in 1966.

58. Utley, a mile northward of the town, was developing as a residential suburb when this photograph was taken about 1900. To the old hamlet of Low Utley, and the few buildings along the Keighley and Kendal Turnpike Road, had been added a Congregational Chapel (1872) and a Board School (1877); succeeding decades were to fill meadows and hillsides with betterclass dwellings. Here we see solid terraced housing on the left, substantial detached homes on the higher ground to the right, their gardens still raw; whilst the adjacent land is ripe for building. Since 1857 Utley had accommodated the town's cemetery – its graves are visible amongst the trees – which doubled as a recreational amenity: before the introduction of parks, the public took pleasure in 'walking round the cemetery'.

Fell Lane Bottom

Keighley

59. Fell Lane is typical of much of Keighley's late Victorian suburban housing – the population rose from 21,859 in 1861 to 41,564 in 1901. Many of the houses in this area were built by the Keighley Industrial Co-operative Society Limited, whose enterprises in the 1890s included stores, a farm, newsrooms, a restaurant and a pork pie bakery. Knowle Park Congregational Chapel, on the left, had opened in 1897. Postcards like this – prosaic yet graphic – were produced in large numbers by small shopkeepers. Amos Dewhirst had started up as a newsagent, stationer and tobacconist in 1899 in nearby Oakworth Road: a keen photographer, he developed a side-line in local views.

60. Old Stockbridge and the River Aire. The bridge was built in 1671 and widened in 1754 when it carried 'a great and common high road leading between Lancashire and Yorkshire'. It was replaced by a sleeker, straighter ferro-concrete bridge between 1928 and 1930. The rural nature of the hillside beyond – Morton Banks – is deceptive, as the area had been extensively mined for coal up to the mid-1800s. When Morton Banks and adjoining Riddlesden were being developed for housing between the wars, advertising brochures painted glowing pictures of the constant sunshine, rich gardens, orchards overflowing with apples, pears and plums, and superior health of the residents in this desirable side of town!

61. A laden barge on the wintry Leeds and Liverpool Canal at Riddlesden in the 1920s. Keighley's position in the Aire Gap ensured its proximity to the canal, the Bingley to Skipton stretch of which was completed in 1773 – an event celebrated with 'bonfires, illuminations, and other demonstrations of joy', plus the half-price selling of the first two boat-loads of coal. Such communications were to encourage development during the Industrial Revolution, although Keighley's nearest wharves were at Stockbridge, a mile out of town. A proposal in 1819 to construct a branch canal into Keighley proper came to nothing – amongst other complications, this would have involved a twelve-arched aqueduct.

62. The southern approach to Keighley railway station in the 1870s, showing on the right a train on the Midland line, which had reached Keighley in 1847, swinging in past the Midland Tool Works. On the left, the Worth Valley Railway, opened in 1867, runs out past the impressive Low Mill and across the River Worth. Prior to 1883, the railway station (which here lurks unseen in the haze beyond the meeting of the two lines) occupied a site on the farther side of Bradford Road. At the time of this photograph, Low Mill was operated by worsted spinners and manufacturers J. and J. Craven, who in this and their other factories, Walk Mill and Dalton Mills, employed more than 2,000 people.

63. Keighley station staff in the earlier 1900s, including the lad and the cat, nursed by the railway policeman. The Midland Railway had come to Keighley in 1847, but the station was re-sited and rebuilt in 1883, in time for the Great Northern Railway which also arrived the following year. For half a century, indeed, Keighley station boasted two sets of staff, the Midland and the Great Northern, which resulted in two booking-offices until 1934 when the Midland assumed overall responsibility. Together with the Worth Valley branch, this made for a busy station. Its amenities featured both first and second-class waiting-rooms. In 1915 there were nearly 120 train departures every weekday, and 42 on Sundays.

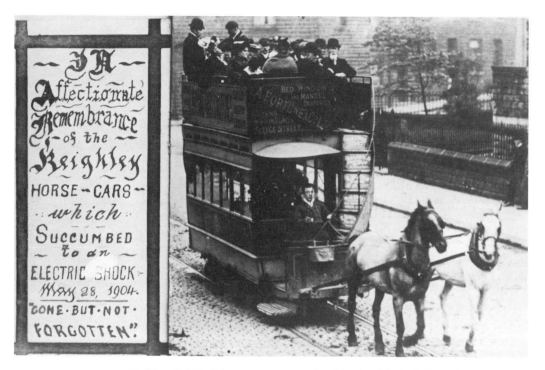

64. When Keighley's horse-trams were replaced by electricity in 1904, local postcard producer G. Bannister marketed this witty epitaph 'in Affectionate Remembrance of the Keighley Horse-Cars which Succumbed to an Electric Shock'. This photograph illustrates both the spartan conditions in which the drivers worked, and the casual dress of the conductor collecting fares on what seems an over-crowded upper deck. At the time of their demise, Keighley's tramcars were drawn by a total of thirty horses, in four shifts. Appealingly, their names have survived. Fourteen were mares: Star, Janet, Nell, Dot, Bell, Queen, Molly, Kitty, Dinah, White-legs, Kendal, Biddy, Susan and Lucy. The rest were: Bob, Major, Billy, Buck, Sweep, Joss, Prince, Sullivan, Briton, Harry, Hawk, Pilot, Jack, Sam, Mick and Tom. Within four days of electrification, they had all been auctioned off, together with their harness, six tram-cars and other equipment, for £804.

BOARD OF TRADE INSPECTION.

MAYOR & COUNCILLORS.

65. Changes in public transport have always occasioned commemorative postcards. Here Major W. Pringle and Mr. A.P. Trotter, experts on behalf of the Board of Trade, inspect the electrified Keighley Corporation Tramways in October 1904, accompanied by the Mayor and Town Councillors. The new service carried 3,589 passengers on its first day – and caused two minor accidents! The cars were made by the Brush Electrical Engineering Company, of Loughborough. Painted in white and crimson livery and originally open-topped, all had covers fitted between 1910 and 1912. Within a few years, Keighley's electric trams were having to compete with motor-buses and tracklesses.

66. A tramcar making one of its final journeys at Utley in 1924. Keighley Corporation had operated frequent electric tram services between Ingrow, Stockbridge and Utley since 1904, in conjunction with various motorbus routes since 1909 and tracklesses since 1913, but in 1924 the trams were phased out. That summer, between June and August, Skipton Road was reduced to half its normal width during repairs and erection of trolley standards; accordingly, for their last weeks on this route, trams were confined to a single track for both directions – a six-minute journey often took twenty. On the right of this photograph is the Roebuck Inn, which had served as a terminus since horse-tram days.

67. This Old Bar House stood in Bar House Lane at Utley. Historically, this rural scene is deceptive, for from 1782 to 1825 Bar House Lane served as a portion of the important Keighley and Kendal Turnpike Road, when tolls were collected here. The Old Bar House survived the re-routing of the turnpike along Skipton Road, to become a picturesque but rather less than idyllic dwelling. Surprisingly, the boundary between the Keighley Borough and the Keighley Rural District ran through the middle of this house, necessitating both authorities having to take out demolition orders in 1932.

68. Members of the Keighley Cycling Club pose outside their wooden headquarters in Bradford Road in their early days. Some are wearing their official uniform of 'navy blue with blue and white shoulder straps'. The Keighley Cycling Club was founded in 1884 with the objects of 'drawing together in fellowship the cyclists in the town and district', organising weekly runs and holiday tours. By 1895 they were floating themselves as a limited company, with 150 share-holders; and it says much for their strength and initiative that their members immediately subscribed the capital for building a handsome new club premises in Cavendish Street. Already, however, they were moving away from simple cycling, for their Cavendish Street club included social, billiards, reading and conversation-rooms.

69. A striking example of mill-owning philanthropy: Mr. James Ickringill's Brass Band outside his residence, Balcony House up Oakworth Road. Mr. Ickringill, of Eastwood Mills, Keighley, and Legrams Mills, Bradford, benefactor of the Oakworth Road Primitive Methodist Mission, founded his Good Lads' Brigade in 1911. Its members pledged to attend Sunday School, say their prayers and refrain from smoking. This code of conduct bore fruit during the Great War, when former Good Lads, successfully resisting various temptations, wrote appreciative letters to Mr. Ickringill. The Brass Band grew out of the Good Lads' Brigade. Mr. Ickringill provided their instruments and a room to practice in. They performed at church and school festivals and galas.

70. In 1876 a small cottage hospital was opened on the Highfield side of Keighley, in a house rented for £75 a year. It had eight beds and a matron with one young girl to help her. Patients could be expelled if 'using profane or abusive language, or guilty of improper conduct, or using spirituous liquors'; whilst operations were performed on a former kitchen table. In fact, this represented the start of a prestigious hospital. Following decades witnessed a series of extensions and improvements, the name Victoria Hospital being adopted in honour of the Queen's 1897 Jubilee. By 1922, more than 15,000 patients were being treated in a single year. During the Great War, as an Auxiliary, Victoria Hospital dealt with nearly 2,000 military cases. it was demolished in 1972.

Morton Banks Hospital, Keighley No. 1027

71. Situated in extensive grounds 'on the sunny slope of Rumbalds Moor', Morton Banks Fever Hospital opened in 1897. During the Great War it was placed at the disposal of the military, the accommodation of its stone-built wards being greatly increased by extra structures of asbestos and creosoted wood. Between wards were 'ashphalted winding paths, flanked by evergreens, flowery bowers and shady seats', as seen in this postcard. The adjoining Leeds and Liverpool Canal provided a bonus in the shape of rowing boats from Whitby for convalescent soldiers, and a motor launch from Windermere for the more gravely wounded. Between 1915 and 1919, Keighley War Hospital and its Auxiliaries dealt with a total of 13,214 military cases. Twenty years later, during the Spanish Civil War, Morton Banks Hospital accommodated Basque refugee children. This also was demolished in 1972.

72. These new recruits, on their way to Keighley railway station in November of 1915, are going down Cavendish Street, passing the Palace Cinema. Like other towns, Keighley had raised many volunteers for the services in the early months of the Great War, but by 1915 numbers were dwindling. These men enlisted during a recruiting boom late that year, severally encouraged by a morale-boosting visit of the London Caledonian Pipe Band and the approaching implementation of Lord Derby's scheme and eventual conscription. 'Men of a high physical standard and excellent character have come forward,' stated the local paper; but significantly the Royal Army Medical Corps and the Army Ordnance Corps had recently extended their upper enlistment age limit to 45 years.

73. A variety of working-class fashion is demonstrated in this margarine queue outside the Co-operative Society's Central Stores in Brunswick Street in 1917. Clogs substantially outnumber boots. In 1917, Keighley's food economy attracted the attention of the national press. Flower-beds in the parks were replaced with potatoes, cauliflowers and cabbages, part of the golf links went under oats, the Trade School boys dug up their football field, and school classes were taken outdoors for lessons on wild edible green-stuffs. 'Keighley,' declared the 'Daily Dispatch', 'is believed to hold the record for economy in this country.' The introduction of food rationing was to improve the lot of shoppers like these.

74. Providing a poignant survey of residents in a not untypical cul-de-sac, George Street celebrates the close of the Great War. Noticeably they consist of women, children and old men. Their slogans include 'God Bless Our Heroes', 'Well Done, Boys', 'Welcome Home', 'Peace at Last', and 'England for Ever', whilst flags of the Allies alternate with the Union Jack. At least one hanging betrays the town's strong Irish element. Keighley's 1914-1918 Roll of Honour lists more than nine hundred names, out of a population of 43,490 at the 1911 Census; and the maimed were to be a prominent sight for years to come.

75. The Town Hall Square soon became a focal point, a location for patriotic and fund-raising events during the Great War. Here, Mayor F.W.L. Butterfield and members of the War Bonds and War Savings Committee pose before a scouting biplane, one of the attractions of Submarine Week in March, 1918. The plane had been brought by road from a Yorkshire airfield. It proved enormously popular. Schoolchildren who bought War Savings Certificates during the week were given tickets allowing them to inspect it 'at close quarters'. The Town Hall Square was decorated with bunting and illuminated each evening by 'a multitude of electric lamps'. Punctually at nine o'clock, bugles sounded 'Lights Out!' and the Borough Band played the National Anthem and all the lights were switched off. The biplane was then guarded all night by men of the Volunteer Force. Keighley Submarine Week raised a grand total of £556,089.

76. These children, enjoying the visit of a pony-drawn carousel about 1920, look healthy enough, but records of the Keighley Medical Officer of Health suggest a different story. Examinations of sample school entrants in 1919 showed 22.6% suffering from defective nutrition, 43.6% with enlarged tonsils, and 28.5% with disorders of the lungs. 33.1% of school leavers had vermin or nits on their heads, and 48.8% had more than four teeth decayed. Height and weight of half-timers – 'a state of affairs which puts an extra strain upon their physique at a time when it is little able to meet the demand' – was found to be below the national standard.